W.A.R. Stories!

Wisdom Acquired Randomly

What you need to know before you get to the airport!

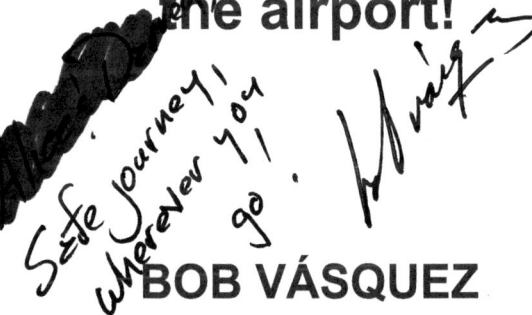

Safe journey!! wherever you go.

BOB VÁSQUEZ

WAJBOOK PRESS

W.A.R. Stories! (Wisdom Acquired Randomly): What you need to know before you get to the airport!

Bob Vásquez

Published in the U.S.A. by Wajbook Press, San Antonio, TX.
Paperback Version: ISBN 979-8-9867720-6-6
Kindle Version: ISBN 979-8-9867720-9-7
Library of Congress Control Number: 2023950027

For information about special discounts for bulk purchases or speaking opportunities, please contact us at bobvasquez@bobvasquez.com.

The views expressed in this book are solely those of the author.

Contents

Foreword 7

Introduction 9

Dedication 11

About the Author 13

Thanks! 15

Why Fly? 17

Safe Journey! 19

My First Flight 21

Before You Go 23

Where to Buy Tickets 25

Make a List 27

There's an App for That 29

The Airlines Are Not Your Friends 31

Kindness is Universal 33

Flying is Stressful 35

At the Airport 37

Only Two Emotions 39

Be Courteous and Kind 41

It's the Small Things 43

Why do Pilots Wear Hats? 45

First Impressions Last 47

Don't You Know Who I Am? 49

Food Prices 51

Airport Bathrooms   53
Make Sure There's Toilet Paper in
    the Stall BEFORE you go in! 55
What Did She Say?   57

Do This   59
Ya Gotta be on Time   61
Follow Directions   65
Carry-Ons   67
Put Your Mask on FIRST   73
Mark Your Bags   75
Where Did I Park?   77
Drop Off or Pick Up   79

Don't Do This   81
Don't be Stupid!   83
Don't Talk to Your Neighbor   85
No Cell Phones, Please   87
Are You Talkin' to ME?   89
Don't Cut the Line   91
Where's the Bathroom?   93

On the Plane   95
Don't Remove Your Shoes   97
Words From the Cockpit   99
Flight Attendants Are People Too 101
Don't Touch the Flight Attendants. 105
What to Wear   107

Don't Lock Yourself in the Lavatory	**109**
Close Your Window	**111**
Don't Kick the Seat	**113**
Don't Hoard the Armrest	**115**
Wear Headphones	**117**
If You're Taking a Pet	**119**
Where's My Bag?	**121**
Aisle or Window Seat?	**123**
Turbulence	**125**
The Value of Duct Tape	**127**
Kids are People Too	**129**
Making Connections	**131**
More Books by Bob	**133**

Foreword

When my Uncle Bob, the author and motivational speaker, asked me to help him with this book and, especially, to write a foreword, I was, literally, speechless. I've never been asked to do this, much less actually done it. Thank you, Uncle Bob, for including me in your project.

I started to recover my words as I read his stories. They're funny, sad, interesting, and true. He's captured many events that happen from preparing to get to the airport to actually being on the plane. I'm pretty sure you'll learn a thing or two, or, at least, you'll be reminded of things you should and shouldn't do. Each of the stories in this book will help make your flight better in one way or another. I promise.

I'm especially grateful for what Uncle Bob says about Flight Attendants since I've been one for a few years as my mother, Patsy, was too. We do what we do for our own reasons but our purpose is always to serve our passengers and to get them to their destinations safely.

As Uncle Bob says, you should read this book BEFORE you get to the airport. Be prepared for what he's telling you will happen, because it will. Maybe not this flight, but sometime. If you can't read it before, then read it while you're in flight. Oh, what the heck, just read it when you can.

I'm honored to play a part in this project and wish you, as Uncle Bob says, a safe journey!

Angie Leigh Beacham

bob vásquez

Introduction

Hi! I'm bob vásquez! I'm an air traveler just like you. I may be different in that I'm a curious observer of life, especially at the airport and in an airplane. Now, I don't collect millions of flying miles every year. But I've flown a few hundred times. I've noticed and reflected on what you're about to read, with the purpose of providing you some tips that may (or may not) make for a better trip.

I've shared these thoughts with a few of my favorite Pilots and my Flight Attendant niece, Angie, who have guided me, educated me, and even laughed at some of my musings. They've validated what I've written. If you can't trust Pilots and Flight Attendants, then, who can you trust?!

All of these observations are true and real. Look around and think about them as you travel and you, too, will agree that they happen all the time. They'll even happen to you.

I hope that you enjoy what you read and that you tell all of your friends, maybe even buy them a copy of the book. Yeah, I'm hoping that what I share with you makes a positive difference in your travels, but I would also love to be able to afford to fly first class, at least once in my lifetime.

Safe journey!

bob vásquez!

bob vásquez

Dedication

This book is dedicated to my late sister-in-law, Patsy Weaver, whom I still love dearly. She was crazy! Not literally, just did stuff many of us wish we could do but didn't have the guts to do them. She approached life at full throttle. She had one speed and that was all the way. She served as a flight attendant for more than 17 years. I, and the entire family, and everyone who knew her, still miss her.

Here are some stories that illustrate what I just said above.

Patsy was working a flight and dealing with severe turbulence. There was an elderly gentleman on the flight, around 80 years of age. He was persistent in wanting coffee and Patsy tried telling him it wasn't safe to serve it. Finally, Patsy told him that she would get him some. She poured it, but as she handed it to him, the plane hit bad turbulence so the coffee spilled all over the man's lap. Without thinking, she grabbed a handful of napkins and started patting him dry. Then it hit her. She suddenly realized the area that she was patting dry. She was so embarrassed that she hid behind another Flight Attendant as he exited the plane. But she laughed about it afterward and suggested that it was probably the most excitement he'd had in a long time.

This was before 9-11 when you could just walk freely around the airport. Her crew room where she had to check in for the flight was near the carousel. There was a man hurriedly walking by with his bag. He brushed by her. As he tossed his bag onto the carousel, there was a hook that slung from it that ended up going under her dress and catching it and ripped her dress open and put her on her back. She was screaming, trying to get the man to realize his bag had caught her. She was screaming so loudly that they shut down the area because they didn't know what was happening. When she was able to get up and get to the crew room, they didn't let her leave to go home and get a new uniform on. They gave her a loaner she said was two sizes too big. And she carried on with her flight hoping the big dress didn't fall off her. One of the Flight Attendants said that when they got to the plane and heard what had happened, they knew it had to be Patsy who was involved.

We love you, Patsy!

About the Author

Bob Vásquez served in the United States Air Force for 50 years, 31 on active duty and 19 as a civilian instructor at the United States Air Force Academy. He retired on 28 February 2022.

A wisdom seeker, storyteller, musician, public speaker, life coach, and mentor, Bob considers his greatest accomplishments the successful raising of his daughters, Tesa and Elyse, six grandchildren, two sons-in-law, and growing closer to Debbie, his lovely bride of more than 45 wonderful and fulfilling years.

Bob is the author of *Heirpower! Eight Basic Habits of Exceptionally Powerful Lieutenants*, *So Ya Wanna Be THE Chief?!*, *S.S.G.T!*, *The College Freshman's Beyond Survival Guide!*, *What I Learned from Dad Made Me a Better Man!*, *The Power Of SUPERvision!*, *Beyond the Little Blue Book*, *A Different Shade of Blue*, and several other books, all available on amazon.com and Apple books.

Connect with Bob at
bobvasquez@bobvasquez.com.

bob vásquez

Thanks!

HUGE thanks to the many folks who had something to do with the writing of this book, including all of the folks with whom I've traveled and have observed at the airport. You didn't realize you were having an impact, ha?! But you do, all the time!

BIG props to Angie, Patsy, Angie's colleagues, all of my pilot friends, and, especially to the folks who make things happen behind the scenes so that we can have safe flights, including airplane maintainance crews, ticket agents, Gate Keepers, airplane cleaning crews, airport maintenance crews, duct tape companies, baggage handlers, and air traffic controllers. You know who you are. I have no idea who you are. But I'm grateful for what you do.

Thanks to my lovely bride of 45 wonderful and fulfilling years for putting up with all of my trips. I know you miss me when I'm gone and thanks for making those lists of reasons that you missed me. I'll get to all of those items soon. Promise!

Last and most, THANK YOU, Creator, for all you bless me with. I'm not worthy, but I'm grateful!

bob vásquez

Why Fly?

Is flying better than driving? You'll have to decide that for yourself but here are some things to consider as you make that decision. Google says….

Opt for driving if:
- You dislike the crowds, lines, and wait times at airports.
- You have a fear of flying.
- There are some great road stops along the way.
- You enjoy driving.
- You will need a car at your destination to get from place to place on your itinerary.
- The drive time is compatible with your ideal vacation time.
- It is better for your budget (more on this below).

Opt for flying if:
- Your kids will get restless on a long car trip.
- You'll spend more time driving than you will at your destination.
- You enjoy flying and it fits with your budget.
- You need to get somewhere ASAP and driving isn't fast enough.

The risk for fatalities and injuries to families is significantly greater on the roads than in airplanes, according to the FAA. Last year, nearly 43,000 people died on America's highways as compared to 13 on commercial flights.

"Statistics show that families are safer traveling in the sky than on the road," said FAA Administrator Marion C. Blakey. "We encourage the use of child safety seats in airplanes. However, if requiring extra airline tickets forces some families to drive, then we're inadvertently putting too many families at risk."

Now, there will surely be times when flying is best and when driving is best. I haven't done it yet, but I hope to one day rent an RV, load up Deb, our dogs, and my daughters' families and take a road trip. I've watched the movies, and it seems like a fun thing to do. I don't ever intend to gather everyone, especially my dogs, and fly anywhere. So far, we Americans are free to do whatever we want, as far as traveling is concerned. That's a blessing.

If you choose to fly, read this book first!

Safe journey!

Safe Journey!

My most favoritest British saying is "Safe journey." I learned it from my friends, Peter and Pam Stockdale, whom we used to visit in England while my family and I were stationed in Germany. Great people, they are. That phrase seems poetic and sincere, which is why I say it so often.

The internet describes it as such: The idiom "have a safe journey" is used to convey well-wishes for a person's travels. The phrase indicates the hope that the individual's trip will be without mishap or danger, whether they're traveling by car, train, airplane, or any other means of transportation. Sometimes, the flight is just a means to a greater end. Wishing someone a "safe journey" implies that the destination is just as important as the voyage itself.

Safety first and always. We may complain about small, and even big, inconveniences while traveling, especially by commercial air, but I'd rather be late than dead. I always hope, and expect, the crews to be conscientious of the aircraft's, crew's, weather, etc, viability BEFORE we take off. If we have to wait a few minutes, but it's important for the safety of the flight, I'm good with that.

One of the most inconvenient flights I had was one November when a colleague of mine, Greg Tate, and I were flying to Texas out of Colorado Springs. It had been icing, not snowing, icing, all night so that when we got on the aircraft, the maintenance crews de-iced and de-iced the plane and the runway for a very long time. They couldn't do it quickly enough for us to take off. I don't remember how long we sat on the plane before the weather changed enough to take off safely, but, as inconvenient as it was, I was okay with it. We, eventually, did take off and we arrived safely at our destination. Safety first and always!

"Journey" is the poetic part of the phrase. It not only refers to the trip you're about to make, but all that goes with it and beyond. I envision a journey such as Homer's *The Odyssey* or Cervantes' *Don Quixote,* maybe even Kerouac's *On The Road,* when I travel. Yeah, I'm kind of a romantic but I'm a storyteller, too. Okay, maybe we don't want to experience all that the characters experience in those books, but I'd rather think of a plane trip as an interesting learning experience that makes me a better person. Hey! I can dream, can't I?

As you read these thoughts and stories you'll probably notice that I sign off each with "Safe journey!" Wherever you go, I sincerely wish you safe and enjoyable travels. As the plane lands at the end of every flight I ever take, I say a little prayer of thanks and that everyone of my fellow passengers and the plane's crew get to their destinations safely and soundly. Ok, soundly may be a stretch for the flight attendants depending on how we passengers behaved during the flight. I hope that you're blessed with a good trip, good health, and happiness.

Safe journey!

My First Flight

I remember my first airplane ride as if it was yesterday. It was in August of 1968. I'd spent my summer in California with my Tío Rulie and Mama Joyce. I'd worked throughout the summer at the Lincoln and Knott Carwash. Man, was that ever hard work, but it was worth it. I boarded that airplane at LAX with $700 in my pocket. Seven crisp 100 dollar bills. I'd never had that kind of money, much less in my pocket. I flew into ELP (El Paso, Texas) where my mom and sisters picked me up and drove us all home to Deming, New Mexico.

I can still feel the exhilaration of that take off. I don't have any idea how fast we were going when we lifted up off the ground but it felt like at least a thousand miles per hour and as if we were headed straight up. I know it wasn't so, but that's how it felt. I don't remember any more about that flight so it must have been smooth and uneventful after that. I loved it!

I got to fly a little during my fifty years in the Air Force. I'm not sure when it lost its glamor and excitement. It eventually became a necessity more than a novelty. I suppose most things do. It eventually evolved into a learning tool as I became more observant of people, events, and processes, at least enough to write this book. I know you're grateful for that. Nowadays, I don't dislike flying, but I do it more for convenience than enjoyment. I usually have to get there fast and flying is the fastest way. I always

dreamed of Scotty beaming me there, but then he died....
Safe journey!

Before You Go

bob vásquez

Where to Buy Tickets

Back in the day, all you had to do was call, on a telephone, a travel agent and they'd guide you through the process of selecting airlines, dates, times, routes, seating, food, just about anything you needed to make the trip. Now, it's on you, my friend! My best advice is Google it.

Think about the questions you have first, then type them into a search engine on the web and you'll get all sorts of responses. There's an app for that. You may go directly to the airline you think you want to fly on or generic sites that include a lot of different airlines and what they offer. ALWAYS read the small print to make sure you get what you pay for and that you don't pay for stuff you don't need. One great resource is your friends who have flown before. Don't be shy. They did the same thing the first few times they flew. Experience is the best teacher when it comes to flying.

You can go online to ask what day and what time is the best time to purchase tickets. You won't get the same answer from everyone, but it may give you a window of opportunity that will help you keep the costs down. And, again, be careful what you sign up for. If you don't understand, ask someone. You'll read this again, but the airlines are not your friends. They exist to make money. They're a business, so be aware of what you're paying for before you push the "purchase" button.

Once you've purchased your tickets, go with it. You can second-guess yourself to death. I coulda so-

and-so. Maybe I shoulda so-and-so. You made the best decision you could with the information you had. Don't worry. Be happy!
Safe journey!

Make a List

You WILL forget something. Trust me! It may be insignificant, until you realize that it's not, but It will happen to you. I DO hope it's insignificant, like your toothbrush (you can buy another one) or deodorant (you can bathe a lot more than usual) or your favorite pen (borrow someone's). My point is that you'll forget something. You WILL!

How do you avoid it happening often? Make a list! When you decide to go on the trip, even before you book your flights (add booking your flights to the list) write down all the stuff you might possibly need or need to do or need to take with you. It's kinda like brainstorming. Don't judge. You cand do that later. Write it down. And DON'T think that you'll remember, so you don't have to write it down. WRITE IT DOWN. Or if you're too sophisticated for that, or weren't taught how to write in school (kinda like opposites, ha?) capture it on your smart phone.

Once you start making arrangements for your trip, you can cross off what you've done and just leave what you thought you might need to add to the list but really didn't. It's much better to be safe than sorry. If you're a guy, you will fight me on this. I know. I am one. And I fight myself on this all the time. Or I did, until I realized that I'm right. If you're married, ask your wife to hold you accountable. And listen to her without fighting. It's for your own good, Man. You may, or may not, appreciate her when you realize that you would have forgotten that Pepto Bismol without her encouragement.

Oh, BTW, if you're traveling overseas, don't forget your passport!
Safe journey!

There's an App for That

Every airline has its own app. They each provide information about your particular flight. I highly suggest you download it onto your smart phone and activate the "provide updates" button, or whatever it's called on your airline's app. You're welcome!
Safe journey!

This is the Captain speaking…

One of my dear friends, Mark Baroni, who's been a pilot for longer than he'll acknowledge shares these thoughts:

1. Turbulence is an imperfection in the air…it ain't perfect.
2. Don't show up intoxicated to the airplane.
3. Just because the airplane is running late, doesn't give you the excuse to run late.
4. For nervous flyers: Seek out the pilots and chat with them about your nervousness. Pilots are not robots…we are human too and don't like flying in turbulent air.
5. Never touch (anywhere) a flight attendant as they are roaming up and down the aisle providing their service…keep your hands to yourselves.
6. Pilots as, a whole, are ruggedly handsome and charmingly witty…just talk to one…they will definitely tell you.

The Airlines Are Not Your Friends

Regardless of the many marketing schemes and propaganda you read about specific airlines, know this: THE AIRLINES ARE NOT YOUR FRIENDS! They're out to make money. Yeah, they'll keep us safe, but only so that they can make more money on us. I MAY be exaggerating a little, but not a lot.

They'll ALWAYS have a sale that you can't say no to. Say NO to it! Read the small print. I won't tell you which airline I usually fly because Frontier may not appreciate what I'm about to say, but I'm gonna say it, by God!

How about a $20 plane ticket across the country, say from Denver to Tampa. That sounds too good to be true, doesn't it. Oh, it's true, but here's the fine print. You'll need to buy a seat. I've always wondered what would happen if you refuse to. Do you stand the entire flight? Where? You're not allowed to stand in the aisle or at the lavatories. In the little cubby where the flight attendants hang out? In the lavatory? I don't know. I'm not about to find out. Denver to Tampa is a more-than-three-hour flight. I want a seat. So I guess I'll pay for it.

Now, depending on where you want to sit and how compact you can make yourself, it'll cost you different prices. As I write, the cheapest seat is $15. You'll need the help of two flight attendants to uncurl you at the end of the flight and you may need hip surgery soon after the flight. Thirty bucks will get you a fairly decent seat if you're shorter than six feet. My favorite seat is in the exit row. The caveat to getting a seat there is that you have to be willing to do what it takes to evacuate the plane in case of an emergency. No timid pax here, please. And, please, don't sit there if you have a broken arm. You're not going to be able to do your duty with only one arm. And those seats are not cheap. I'm thinking that if the captain drafts me to be a flight attendant, safety being their first priority, then they should pay ME for volunteering.

If you intend to take a bag with you, it'll cost you. "What about one I can put under the seat in front of me?" you ask. It'll cost you. "How about if I stow it above my seat?" It'll cost you. "Okay, I'll check it." It'll cost you. In fact, you're gonna think I'm lying, but I'm not. You know how much it costs to check a bag on that $20 flight? $75! I just looked. Your bag is gonna cost you THREE TIMES more than your plane ticket. And don't be ONE POUND over the weight limit (the bag) when you check in because it'll cost you an ADDITIONAL $100. It just happened to me last month!

What did I tell you? THE AIRLINES ARE NOT YOUR FRIENDS! It's a business, not a service. Now, don't get me wrong. They're not HORRIBLE! At least most of the time, in my experience. Ok, sometimes…. But it's often the best, maybe the only, way to get there, especially if you have to get there quickly.

Back in the day, you'd call a person who would help you work all of this out. Then it got to where you had to pay for that service. I don't use it, but I'm sure it's still available but it'll cost you. It's best to go online and research the best you can to get the best "deal" that you can. Good luck with that!

Safe journey!

Kindness is Universal

I'm on my way back to Fairchild Air Force Base in Washington state. I'm in St Louis and there's a major storm headed our way. Based on the weather predictions for the area, there's no way I'll make it home today. We'll soon be bombarded by rain, hail, very high winds, probably tornadoes, maybe even sharks! AHA! There's an earlier flight going west. I talk with the airline representative about the possibility of taking that to San Francisco then catching a flight to Spokane from there. Almost a good idea, the rep tells me. I'll have to stay the night and catch an early flight north the next morning. I'm okay with that. It'll still get me home early tomorrow, since I have a very important meeting to attend tomorrow afternoon.

I miss the storm en route to San Francisco. In fact, it's a fairly smooth flight. As I disembark the airplane, an airline representative is there to greet me and tells me where to catch the shuttle to the hotel that the airline will be putting me up in. It's about midnight. I'm a bit tired from a full day of work, then traveling for three hours. I'm grateful and I tell the rep so.

As I sit, waiting for the shuttle, another airline rep approaches me with a lady holding a child in her arms. She asks me if I'm who I am and if I'm headed to the hotel the airline has booked for me. I acknowledge so. Then without me even being able to respond, she hands me a card, bows to the lady, who is obviously of Asian descent, and takes off back into the terminal. I exchange glances with the lady as I read the card that says, "I'm Vietnamese. I don't speak any English. I'm going to the same hotel you are. Please help me." Okaaaayyyy...?! What am I supposed to say? No? No can do. These sorts of things happen to me all the time, so I'm almost used to it.

It's almost amazing how the lady and I communicate. Mostly in gestures. I even speak to her in Spanish. Hey, what's the difference? She doesn't understand that either.

We both get to the hotel safely. I check in and make sure she and her child check in, too. All goes well. We exchange bows as we go our separate ways. The next morning, as I check out of the hotel, I ask the receptionist about the lady and her baby. She tells me that she's already gone to catch her flight and that she asked the receptionist to thank me for helping her.

We don't even have to speak the same language to help each other out. Surely, you've had the opportunity to help a stranger. You don't know their circumstances and maybe that's none of your business. Your business, my business, is to make a positive difference in someone's life. When that opportunity arises, accept it. Be kind. It's amazing the impact that might have.

Safe journey!

Flying is Stressful

Watch the movie *Home Alone* to give you an idea of how stressful flying can be. You may be a very organized person and the people you're traveling with may be trained to follow your every order, but it will get stressful nonetheless.

Knowing this, itself, may calm you down a little bit. Maybe not. Depending on who you're traveling with and how much THEY'RE pinging. Things happen. No matter how well you've planned your trip, something out of the realm of your thinking might, or will, happen. You may have read that popular meme that states, "Be Calm." That's as close to the remedy as you might get.

Believe it or not, breathing is critical in helping you get through all of the craziness of flying. Whenever you get to the point that you want to hit someone or puke, take a few minutes alone, close your eyes, and breathe deeply. Bad stuff out, good stuff in. It can't hurt. Don't stand next to a trash can when you do this. Trust me. You're welcome.

Consider this, there are 150 other people on that plane trying to get to some destination that's probably not the same one that you're trying to get to. Maintenance, crew, weather, all sorts of influences will be coming at you, plus those 150 people, all at once. You're all in the fray together. So, again, stay clam.

I was going to say that it could be worse. I don't want to jinx your trip. It could get worse.

Safe journey....

From a Flight Attendant

First of all, it should be illegal to make us get out of bed before the sun comes up. No normal human being can function this early. (Sips coffee.) So, I get on the plane at this ungodly hour and I'm trying to check my PA. (Picks up receiver and blows) Nothing. (Blows again.) Nothing. (Looks at phone and makes sure it's not falling apart and blows again.) Still nothing. (Stares at phone some more, then realizes that I have my dang mask on, and I actually need to form words.) It's too early for this!

What you need to know before you get to the airport!

At the Airport

bob vásquez

Only Two Emotions

My favorite pastime at the airport, other than waiting, is watching people. It's almost amazing what you might see, especially if you pay attention. As Yogi Berra said, "You can observe a lot by watching."

It seems to me that there are only two emotions expressed at the airport, sadness and happiness. There's no neutral. Okay, maybe people who fly for business purposes have been desensitized to the fun and excitement of flying, but otherwise people are sad or happy there.

I can feel deep sadness as I write, based on my experiences of dropping my family members off at the airport, particularly our daughter, Elyse, and her family. Deb and I took Elyse to the airport many times during the time that she attended college. I can still see her taking the escalator down to the tram at DEN. My heart breaks when I think about it, so I try not to. Now, there are four munchkins who accompany her, which makes it four times tougher. Five when her husband, Jeremy, is with them. The good thing is that I have to drive home so that redirects my heart to the task of driving on I-25 with all the crazies who are let out to distract me. I guess I should appreciate them.

On the other hand, I can hardly sleep when I know that I have to pick up my White Clan at DEN. (They're my White Clan because Jeremy's last name is White. Hey! I'm no racist!) The hardest part is that I usually can't get to their arrival gate because of security reasons. But I can almost feel all of those little arms around my neck and their shouting out "Opa!" as loudly as they can.

Yeah, those are the two emotions, sadness and happiness. Watch for them while you're waiting for your plane or an arrival. I always say a prayer for those who are leaving their loved ones. I pray for their loved ones' smooth and safe flight and that those who left them return to their normal lives quickly, and that they are blessed with seeing each other again soon.

I also pray for those who are reunited. That they may appreciate their newly found time together and that they show their love for each other as much as possible. Life is too short not to do that, and now's their opportunity.

Safe journey!

Be Courteous and Kind

Be courteous and kind. Everyone is in a hurry. That is all….
Safe journey!

From a Flight Attendant

This is what was actually said and how I felt. "To my fellow colleagues, as I sit waiting to commute home minding my own business a pax makes a comment to me that "Flight Attendants are Glorified Waitresses." Please send someone to Terminal C with "Aviation First Responder" equipment to revive this pax. Thanks in advance.

It's the Small Things

I'm sitting on the airport shuttle waiting to get to the airport for my flight out. I'm running late and the buss is full. As I look around, it seems everyone is running late. A lot of anxious faces looking at each other. Just as we're about to take off, a little old lady barely gets on. She looks just like my Abuela, my grandma! She gets on the bus and looks around. No seats anywhere. As I said, the buss is full. I hear a little voice telling me, "I am an American Airman. I am a Warrior!" I can't help but offer the little old lady, Abuela, my seat. She accepts. She smiles at me as she sits down.

Man, there's so much traffic this morning! Will we make it to our flights on time? It's slow going all the way. We finally arrive at the airport. Chaos explodes as everyone on that bus starts to rush out the doors. There's that little voice again, "I am an American Airman. I am a Warrior! Guardian! Sentry! I protect my country with my life. I will never leave an American behind!" I can't help but stand guard over Abuela.

Everyone gets off the bus except Abuela and me. She smiles, looks me in the eye, and says, "You're a good man, Son." Abuela called me Mijo-Son.

Am I gonna make my flight? It's late! Now I have plenty of time. I sit down and think about what just happened. "You're a good man," Abuela, the little old lady, said. What a compliment! And all because I did a few small things any Warrior would do. I was courteous and considerate and I protected her when she couldn't protect herself.

We often think about character being measured in big things. But we seldom do big things. Our character is measured in the little things that we do on a daily basis. In this lady's mind, and heart, I hope, I measured up to being a good man. That's a big thing to be.

Safe journey!

Why do Pilots Wear Hats?

I served in the United States Air Force for 50 years. I wore a hat all of those years. Outdoors. It was required. You could actually go to jail if you didn't. I don't think that ever happened, but it was possible.

Almost interestingly, I still wear a hat. After 50 years you kinda continue with old habits, but there's another reason. It started way before I joined the Air Force. My grandfather, Firpo, who grew up in the very old, stern Mexican culture, wore a hat. A fedora. I thought that he hated me because he always expected me to live up to his standards and forced me to when he could. Men wearing a hat was one of those standards. I rebelled until I joined the Air Force. And then they made me wear a hat! Karma, I guess....

Since then, for most of my life, I've been observant of hats and men who wear them. Women, too, but I see a lot less of them than I do men. I ask this question of myself every time I'm in an airport, "Why do pilots wear hats? Indoors." They take them off once they're in the cockpit.

It can't be a status thing, can it? *Hey, look, everyone! I'm wearing a hat inside the building. That means that I'm a pilot.* Now, female pilots wear hats, too. I've seen it. That doesn't make anymore sense. Maybe breaking the glass ceiling isn't all it's cut out to be. *Yes, ma'am, you'll be authorized to wear a hat inside the airport if we hire you to fly for us. It's a great perk.* (Great excitement exudes from the female pilot candidate at hearing this!)

45

I did the research. I Googled it. The reason pilots wear hats is, well, here's what the web said, "Many airlines still require their pilots to wear hats for the same reasons that they require their pilots to wear a uniform; recognition, authority and professionalism."

I can see a uniform doing that, but a hat? Indoors? I dunno…. Evidently, there are some pilots who refuse to wear hats. I'm not sure I'm willing to fly with them. I mean, what authority would they still have? And what if not wearing a hat does affect their professionalism? I want MY pilots to be professionals in everything they do. A hat will guarantee that, I'm sure.

Safe journey!

First Impressions Last

Seems like a hundred years ago that we were allowed to go up to a person's departure gate without having to go through any security. If you remember that, you're probably old. I know I am!

I was heading back to base after visiting my family in New Mexico. The nearest airport was in El Paso, Texas, a little over 100 miles away. My mom and sisters carried me to the airport to see me off. As I just mentioned, since times were different then, we went up to the gate that led to the airplane I'd be taking to wherever I was stationed at the time.

That airport has been renovated a few times so what I'm about to describe isn't the way it is now. I noticed that there were no doors anywhere in the building. Anywhere! I looked for them. We're sitting at the gate when, all of a sudden, the wall in front of us moves. It opens up. It's a giant door. And people come out of it. Including the pilot of my flight.

I often suggest to audiences that first impressions last. Man, did that guy ever make a first impression. A bad one! He looked like he'd slept in his uniform. It was all wrinkled, which, by the way, was a huge no-no in my family. I couldn't tell if he had combed his hair, but it protruded from underneath his hat like octopus tentacles. His hat was on the back of his head about to fall off. Needless to say, he just didn't look very professional.

Mom looked at me and asked me, "Is that your pilot?" "Yes, ma'am. I think he is," was my reply.

47

"Change flights!" Mom answered adamantly. "What?" I asked befuddled. "Change flights, Mijo. You're not flying with that guy!" Mom admonished me. I was afraid that she'd soon get out her chancla, right there in front of everyone, so I changed flights. I took a later one.

First impressions do last. Forever! I still remember that incident as if it happened earlier today. My daughter, Tesa, has always admonished me to not judge a person by their cover, and I strive to give everyone I meet an opportunity to impress me in a positive way, but it's a human trait to make up our minds about people when we first see them. In his book, *Blink*, Malcolm Gladwell says that people make up their minds about others within three seconds. That's fast. I always wonder, "Who counted?" Anyway, I think you'll agree that it doesn't take long or much to make an impression, especially a first one. Be aware of that, especially if you aspire to be a professional of some sort, and always put your best foot forward. First impressions last!

Safe journey!

Don't You Know Who I Am?!

As I entered the airport, a lady driving one of those courtesy shuttles stopped me and asked if I needed a ride. "Do I look like I need a ride, Ma'am?" I asked her. "DO YOU KNOW THAT I'M A CHIEF MASTER SERGEANT WHO REFUSES TO USE AN UMBRELLA EVEN WHEN IT'S HAILING? DO YOU KNOW THAT I CAN STILL KICK MOST AIRMEN'S BUTTS, ALTHOUGH IT'LL TAKE ME LONGER THAN IT USED TO? DO YOU KNOW I'M CHIEF BOB VÁSQUEZ?"

She looked at me, a bit startled, and quickly drove off. I didn't realize my gate was at the end of the terminal (some of you have heard or read my "flight from hell" story).

My knees and heels are killing me. Barely made it to the gate. I didn't cry, though...okay, maybe a little. Heading home! Be humble!

Safe journey!

This is the Captain speaking...

My friend, Ryan Gavina, says:

Delays happen. They're not fun for anyone. Don't assume we're not doing what we can to get you where you need to go. Safety is always #1 for the crew and that will always be the first consideration. Also, the cabin crew is doing everything they can to make the flight as safe and enjoyable as possible. A thank you will go a long way.

Food Prices

It used to be that food was a lot more expensive at the airport than outside of it. I don't know if airport food pricing settled down or if outside food prices increased. Nonetheless, there's not a huge difference anymore. As my Flight Attendant niece, Angie, says, "Most places may be one or two dollars higher than the original place but it's about what you'd pay at a movie theater, football or baseball game, concert, or some other special event. For example, a Chick-fil-A meal here in Jacksonville is roughly $9.00 at the restaurant and $10.59 at the airport. However, the drink machines and snack machines in airports are usually cheaper than the gift shops."

As a reminder, you can take SOME food items in you handbag or backpack, but there are restrictions. Know what you can take BEFORE you get to Security. There's an app for that. They'll quickly confiscate what's not allowed.

And, please, eat before boarding. There's little worse than the person in the seat next to you pulling out a Whopper and not offering you a bite! Okay, don't do that. Don't offer it nor accept the offer. That Whopper is going to make the entire plane smell. Good if you dig Whoppers, not if you're a vegan. And, we should all be respectful of others' food allergies. You may not realize that Chick-fil-A chicken is fried in peanut oil. There are people who are allergic to anything peanut. Even the smell.

And don't count on the airlines feeding you. It seldom happens anymore. Sometimes, they'll offer a snack of some kind, but it'll cost you. No more peanuts. Sometimes pretzels. In tiny little bags. I remember when people used to complain about airplane food. There have been plenty of long flights when I've wished I had one of those meals. By the way, nowadays, if you DO purchase a snack you'll have to pay with a card or an app, no more cash. Be prepared.

Safe journey!

Airport Bathrooms

One of the things that often irks me, is the placement of sinks and towel dispensers in airport bathrooms. I don't know if it's just me, but why don't the architects ever think about us customers when they design the bathrooms? Now, it could be that it's just the men's bathrooms that are built without regard for the customer. I don't know what women's bathrooms look like. I've never been in one.

The problem is that they put the sinks and towel dispensers as far away from each other as they can. I'm usually carrying bags of some sort, so I have to decide what to do with them first, then how to wash and dry my hands. There's never a place to put my bags. On the floor? Nope. On the sink? That won't work. Where should I put them so that I can dry my hands? The sinks and towel dispensers should be close enough that I can reach them. Can I get an Amen?!

I'd almost always rather travel by myself than with someone. That way, I can make decisions without having to consult someone else. I've been doing that for decades. It works for me. But I must admit that traveling with Deb was a blessing. She held my bags while I went to the bathroom. Love that kid!

Safe journey!

From a Flight Attendant

And the other part, it sucks not being able to go to the gate! I remember when mom worked at the bank in the airport and dad doing construction I used to go walk around the airport in the summer when school was out. I can recall meeting famous people, Rick Flair being one of them. Just different times. I wish that was still a thing.

Make Sure There's Toilet Paper in the Stall BEFORE You go in!

Remember that saying, "When ya gotta go, ya gotta go!"? It was conceived at an airport. No, REALLY! OK, I don't know, but it might have been. I don't know about you, but THE URGE always hits me at the most inconvenient times at the airport. Naw, I'm good.... Oh, WAIT! We're boarding? Oh, man, I gotta go!

Evidently, it's okay to go when the plane is being boarded. It's rude, though. Go BEFORE you get on the plane. And do so 20 minutes before boarding time. Okay, that suggestion isn't scientifically based, it just seems like 20 minutes before you board should give you enough time to do your business and get back to the gate in time to wait for your group to be called.

And as the title of this thought says, make sure there's toilet paper in the stall BEFORE you go in there. You may be old enough to remember a tagline from a movie titled *Alien* that said, "In space no one can hear you scream." Well, that's kinda how you'll feel if you need toilet paper and there is none there. I mean, what do you do? You can, I suppose, scream, but I bet no one would "hear" you. Come on, a stranger in the airport bathroom yelling for toilet paper? I'm outta there! I didn't hear nuthin.

I'm telling you this because you're not gonna think about it...until it's too late. So, be proactive and check first. You'll thank me the day there's none there. You're welcome.

And safe journey!

From a Flight Attendant

I recall when you had to fly in your "Sunday best." It's crazy the things we see worn, especially during Covid. Girls travel in swimsuits, people travel in pajamas and slippers. I once had a lady come on in hair rollers. People come in costumes, wear all types of masks. We shouldn't judge. I get that. But at least present yourself like you care. I get being comfortable, but you can still look nice and be comfortable.

What Did She Say?

The airport is the place where communication is the key to success. Ya gotta know! A lot of stuff. Yeah, work and other places would claim that distinction, but there's no place that comes close to the airport. The more you know, the better. That's why you're reading this book, isn't it? However, comma, there's a point at the airport where it's imperative that you get the information you need to make your flight, but don't count on getting it....

You will hear plenty of announcements as you traverse the airport toward your gate. You'll be able to hear each commercial clearly, as if the announcer is standing next to you. What you won't hear and who is supposedly sharing critical information with you will be the Gate Keeper. (The person at the gate you're boarding the plane through.) When you get to your gate you'll eventually see an airline representative at the counter next to the actual door that leads to the jetway and to the plane itself.

That person will make announcements about boarding, space available seats, and other critical information that you must have. Trust me, you won't be able to make out what he/she said. I've sat four feet away from said person and still didn't understand a word they said.

I've been a professional musician all of my life. I've worked with singers. Many singers. Some had good microphone technique. They were trained. It was obvious. Many weren't and I had to do just-in-time training to keep them from blowing up the sound guy's ears. Especially tapping on that mic. YIKES!

Well, Gate Keepers are, obviously, not trained at using that little mic. It looks like a CB mic, if you remember those. And I'm convinced that they think that the closer you get to the mic and the louder you speak into it, the easier it will be for pax to hear them. It's just the opposite! If you're a Gate Keeper, please, DON'T DO THAT! Move back off the mic and speak normally. And that means normal tempo. Don't get nervous and speak fast. That'll make it worse. And enunciate properly. You're welcome!

As for being a passenger, you will strain your earballs trying to hear what that person is saying. It won't help. The best thing to do is to ask a fellow passenger what was said. She probably heard the part that you didn't and you can exchange what you heard to make up the complete message.

And DON'T go up and ask what was said. Them's fightin' words! That Gate Keeper will take offense to you challenging their communication ability and won't clarify. Been there. Done that. Failed. By the time you get to your destination, you'll be suffering with ear strain. That's part of flying.

Safe journey!

Do This

bob vásquez

Ya Gotta be on Time

Timeliness is next to godliness. I read that somewhere. There's some truth to that. Especially when you're flying
Timeliness is important to me, especially when I'm traveling. Even if it's on vacation. (I seldom vacation. It's not in my nature.) I set a time when I'm leaving the house and when I intend to be at my destination. The airlines ostensible do the same, but it seldom happens. I don't remember ever taking off on time. Now, we usually land earlier than expected (And, of course, have to wait to get to the gate because there's another plane at it that is late taking off, which makes us late to arrive.).
This ticks me off almost as much as a doctor's appointment. I'll ask for a ten o'clock appointment but I'm expected to arrive 15 minutes early. That, in reality, makes my appointment time 9:45, doesn't it? And the reason for that, actually, there are two, is first, just in case the doctor is running early, which NEVER happens, you don't want to waste her time. As if MY time (I had to take the day off to go to that appointment, which, by the way, it took me months to get.) isn't important. Time IS money, even when you're not a doctor. The other reason is so that you can fill out the papers that they could have, or did, send you online to fill out. Same exact questions. "But I already filled these out online before coming here," I'll argue with the receptionist, who looks at me angrily over her glasses and points me to the waiting area with a clipboard, a pen, and the papers that I have to fill out. Then, guess what? The nurse asks you the

same questions! Maybe they're trying to verify that I'm actually ill and not just wanting to hang out with my proctologist.

For years, and I don't know who or why they decided this, we've been admonished to arrive at the airport two hours before our flight. In some cases that's reasonable. I mean, the crew may have shown up on time and the maintainers may have gotten the plane ready early, so the captain wants to take off early. Let's fly! Yeah, RIGHT!

Now, almost every time I fly, I receive a notice from my airline, via text, to arrive at the airport even earlier since TSA is running late and the security check lines will be long. HIRE MORE PEOPLE! That's what I'd have to do to keep my business viable, or shut down. And don't get me started with TSA!

I always do like to get to the airport early. It helps ease some of the stress of flying. I get there, park my car, check in if needed, get to my gate, go pee, and hang out watching all of the other crazies going through what I'm going through or worse. I especially enjoy watching the folks running on the moving sidewalk, in a rush to catch their flight. "Haha," I think when I see them. "You shoulda heeded the at-least-two-hour-early admonishment and that text message."

I'm pretty sure that all airlines, at least the major ones, now have what they call "early check in." I can check in for my flights 24 hours ahead of time via my computer or my iPhone app for the particular airline I'm flying. Mine even remind me to do that when it's time to check in. It saves a lot of trouble. Especially if you're not checking bags. If all I'm taking with me is my carry-on, I can just get through security and get to my boarding gate pretty quickly. Even if you have to check a bag, most airports have automated systems that make it quicker to get to the gate. UNLESS you're overweight. That's a different issue altogether. Anyway, do what you have to to get to your gate at least on time, but better yet, early.

Then, after all the rush, you'll sit there on the tarmac for a while. Doesn't matter why. They make up the reasons, I'm convinced. But you'll have to hurry up and wait. I served in our Air Force for 50 years. I know how to do that, so I take it in stride. If you're not accustomed to it, get used to it. It'll happen every time. Refer to my "The Value of Duct Tape" story for more on this event.

What I find interesting, and I've done my research, I've done plenty of observation on this, as critical as it seems to get to and through places on time, there are no clocks to be found at the airport! I'm not lying! Next time you're at an airport, try to find a clock, just one. Now there should be some TV monitors that note arrivals and departures. There's a clock on those, but otherwise, try and find one. I guess the folks who design airports figure that if you can afford a plane ticket, you can afford a watch.

I always assume that the airlines care about me so much that they're willing to wait for me in case I get caught up in traffic or have a flat tire along my way to the airport. I mean, that's what they tell me when I call their customer service number. That I'm their best customer. Guess what? They don't. They won't care why you're late. The gate door will close even if you're one minute late. Don't try this at home.

Be on time! I was raised on Lombardi time: If you're 15 minutes early, you're on time. If you're on time, you're late. Now, get out there and hurry up and wait!

Safe journey!

Follow Directions

This one suggestion may be the most difficult of all as you fly the friendly skies. It may be what makes the skies friendly…or not!

Follow directions! Okay, I can sense that you're already arguing, stating that you're an American, you live in America, the home of the free. GET OVER IT!

As you arrive at the airport and, especially, once you're on the plane, look around. Are you the only person in it? Well, actually, I've been the only person in a commercial plane. Yeah, there's a story there. Look for my next book of W.A.R. Stories. Anyway, chances are that there are A LOT of people around you. All going somewhere. In a hurry. That seems to be the case on any flight. Everyone is in a hurry to get to where they think they want to go.

Put yourself in the flight attendant's shoes. Not literally. Read my story about shoes. Your job is to herd all of these cats so that you all can get to your destination safely. Interestingly, evidently, the flight attendant's primary job is to ensure that all of the passengers are safe. Not to bring you drinks and pretzels, not to help you put that oversized carry-on into the bin above your seat, not to calm your crying baby, but to keep you, and everyone else, safe. WOW! That's a tough job. I wouldn't do it. I don't care HOW much it pays. (It doesn't pay as much as it should. I know. I have family members in the business.)

How in the world would you herd those cats in an orderly way. Well, nowadays, it's gotten tougher.

I've recently been on some flights where cops came on board the plane after we landed to arrest folks who didn't do what I'm suggesting you do....Follow directions!

So, let's say that the pilot is alerted that there's turbulence ahead. He/she passes on to the flight attendants that the proper precautions need to be taken. The flight attendant gets on the intercom and alerts everyone that the captain has just turned on the seatbelt sign. Now, please take your seat and buckle up. Simple, right? But people don't/won't do it. The flight attendant will probably have to say it several times. I've been on flights where we're going through some strong bumps and the flight attendant is still trying to get people to take their seats and buckle up. (If you don't, cops may be waiting for you at landing. And rightfully so. I've already mentioned that.)

I've never been on a flight on which the flight attendants mess with you....Sit down. Stand up. Sit down. Now, stand up. Their directions are purposeful. Follow directions! I know I've said that already. Maybe once more?

If nothing else, be respectful of that person, the flight attendant. He or she is just doing their job. And remember, it's about safety. Yours and all of your fellow passengers. Show some respect and kindness. It won't hurt you. In fact, it may help everyone. Follow directions!

Safe journey!

Carry-ons

Airlines offer an option to bring a bag onto the airplane with you. It's called a carry on. Based on my extensive research (I Googled it), on most domestic airlines, "Including handles and wheels, the maximum dimensions for a carry-on are 22 inches long, 14 inches wide, and 9 inches high." Notice the quotation marks. Not MY rules, the airlines' rules. Now, either y'all don't have a tape measure, don't know how to read one, or just don't care. I won't say I fly a lot, but I fly enough to know that most people don't realize that THIS MEANS YOU! I've seen people carry on duffle bags full of stuff that cannot be within those measurements. NO WAY! And they stuff them into the overhead bins. The purpose for those restrictions, again, my research shows, is so that they "will be able to be stored safely in the overhead bin for your flight." Yeah, RIGHT! I've seen people bring on bags that it took the passenger and a couple of flight attendants to stuff into that luggage area. And, of course, it also took all of the space that anyone else was planning to use for their legal-sized bag, so that they have to store it seven rows back. What's omitted in that description is "above YOUR seat." It, pretty quickly, creates a domino effect that's gonna mess everything up, including emotions. I've seen it happen. Okay, it's happened to me! Ticks me off!

Yeah, we live in a culture where we're afraid to confront others, even when they're violating a rule or law. So we let it go. Let someone else deal with it. So, who is supposed to enforce the carry-on rule? I'm thinking it should be the Gate Keepers (They're actually called Gate Agents, but I prefer my description.), but based on my experience and astute observation, they seldom, if ever, enforce those rules. There's even a little metal box with a sign that says, "YOUR carry-on must fit in here or don't carry it on. Check the bag, please." Or something to that effect. No one sticks their bag in there to ensure they meet the requirements.

Now, here's the problem. You have to pay to carry a bag on. I've never seen, nor have I ever experienced, anyone ask a passenger for verification that they paid to bring that carry-on onto the plane. To their credit, I have seen a Gate Keeper tell folks that their carry-on was too large and that they had to check it. Evidently, carry-ons can be any size that you can get away with.

There's also supposed to be a weight limit for that carry-on. I can't say I've personally weighed every extra-large bag I've seen brought on board, but judging by the grunting and straining it took that 300 pound former football player to get that bag in the storage bin, it had to weigh more than the allotted 35 pounds. Had to!

My biggest beef with carry-ons is that folks have no respect or regard for others. It seems as though it's almost a game to see what you can get away with bringing on board.

Oh, and you can also bring a personal item. "Personal items are limited to 17 inches long, 10 inches wide and 9 inches high." Okay, I'm not even going there....

PLEASE...pay for your carry-on if you bring one. Abide by the size and weight limits. Put it where it's supposed to go on the airplane. Be respectful of other passengers' space. We're all in the same boat, okay, plane, together. Let's make it a safe and pleasant journey for all. Thanks for your support. Safe journey!

This is the Captain speaking...

My Chosen Brother, Jason Harris, suggests the following.

My three flying philosophies:
1. Take offs are optional, landings are mandatory.
2. Always make sure your landings equal your take offs!
3. Never, ever Lisa off TSA!

Flying can be stressful for all involved. There are many people who get to fly but they've never flown before. Flying is all new to them and this often times requires patience in the very confusing terminals and in the confines of an airplane. I take pride in my mission as a pilot for many reasons. Our job allows us to be in service to and for humanity. We never know when it's that persons first flight of their life and they're going to say their last goodbye to a loved one. Perhaps it's their first flight and they're going to witness the birth of a child. Perhaps it's their 1,000th flight and they are distraught because they're going to sit with their aging parent who has been given days to live. We never know what people are going through. I do my best to extend a fair measure of grace that I would want. Beyond that, being courteous and courageous enough to demand courtesy for others goes a long way. Traveling is stressful.

As a pilot, I'm no more happy about our delay than you, the paying passenger. I'll do my best to keep you informed, as best I can. I'll never rush a take off if it compromises our safety. If you ever wondered about the safety of the flights, consider that those of us upfront making decisions enjoy life and have families we love just as much as everyone else. We want to make it to our destination and back home safely. We will do our best to get you there but we will never compromise safety. Our job upfront is relatively easy, or at least we make it look that way. It's only easy because of the amount of hours and training that goes into preparing us for each flight. We meticulously plan as many details as possible to include evaluating the weather to give us all as smooth of a flight as possible. Then there are the challenges that are thrown our way that require us to make hundreds of decisions in mere minutes. Imagine calculating how much fuel we have left, in hours and minutes, followed by a descent rate to get us to a safe altitude, while considering where the safest and most efficient place is to land, while ensuring the passengers are safe along with avoiding other airplanes and any other restrictions that we have to abide by. This is just a small preview of what happens when there's an emergency. We train for this continuously. Our job is to be prepared for as many contingencies as possible and to have contingency plans in place, should the fit hit the shan! We also have support agencies on the ground on standby to assist us in the event we have to start exercising our contingency planning.

Don't worry. We've got it!

From a Flight Attendant

If you are flying to a special event, go the day before, or drive. People don't think about things happening like maintenance or weather. Things that can cause delays or cancellations. Also, if you have connecting flights, allow yourself more than an hour, due to the same issues above. I don't know why people book flights with less the 30 minutes to get off a plane and go catch another one. Sometimes the gate agents are tied up and don't get down to connect the jet bridge for people to get off. They get angry at us for their poor planning. I always tell people that more than an hour on domestic and a couple hours for international is good.

Put Your Mask on FIRST

Just before you take off, the flight attendants are going to give you a safety briefing. They all participate in this. Kinda like show and tell in grade school. It's important to listen and watch, particularly if this is your first flight. After your 100th flight, you probably won't listen nor watch anymore.

A couple of things always get me about that safety briefing. First of all, don't we ALL know how to buckle and unbuckle a seatbelt? My three-year-old grandkid buckles and unbuckles his seatbelt without help. Best to be safe than sorry, I suppose.

The flight attendant will get to the part about the little yellow oxygen cup, or mask, falling down in front of you in case the plane loses altitude quickly. The attendant's message is to don the mask on *first*, take care of your kids, and then breathe normally. In that order. (Breathe normally. Yeah, right! If that little yellow cup comes down in front of me, my first reaction will be to breathe as fast as I can—it's somehow associated with Abraham Maslow's hierarchy of needs. Survival is the first need!)

What gets me, and I've done the research, they NEVER EVER mess up The Do when they demonstrate how to don that little yellow mask onto your face. It's like their hair is off limits for that demo. If I had to don that little yellow mask in seconds I, surely, wouldn't care if it messed up my hair.

Now, assuming I even remember that my wife and kids are with me on that flight, I'll certainly make sure that they have their masks on too. My gut tells me that this is especially difficult for moms. Dads are

73

from the old school: "I brought you into this life, and I'll take you out!" Moms will sacrifice *everything* for their children. Men think, "Hey, we'll just have more." (Okay, not really. Okay, maybe.) Anyway, the idea of taking care of yourself first is credible in this situation. It probably won't take you long to don the mask. If that's the only way to breathe, you'll do it with incredible speed.

Rather than encouraging us to breathe normally, I think that the attendant really wants to keep us from panicking. That's one of the vital things you learn in CPR classes—don't panic. Emotional minds cause panic. Once emotion takes over, you can't think logically, and the fight-or-flight instinct takes control—not a good thing. If you take care of yourself first and don't panic, doesn't it make sense that you'll be able to assess what's going on a little bit better and make the right decisions? Then you'll be able to take care of others, including your family.

The point of all of this is that you have to take care of yourself first! Put you mask on FIRST!

Safe journey!

Mark Your Bags

I have a bag or two that I use for flying. I usually purchase them because they do something that makes it more convenient to get around an airport or a plane. Like the wheels that turn every which way. Those are a Godsend! Whoever invented those should be sainted.

I've also purchased some that looked different, that would be easy to spot in an overhead bin or, especially, on a baggage claim carousel. NOT! They all look alike! Or similar. Too similar for you not to mark your bag somehow. I remember getting a hot pink bag for our daughter, Elyse, when she flew back and forth to college. Every college kid must have gotten theirs at the same store that we did.

I've marked mine with name tags that include my name and address in case it gets lost or stolen. As if a thief would return it. "Sir, I stole your bag at the airport. I just thought you might want it back, so here you go." Yeah, THAT'S gonna happen. Some of the name tags I've used are huge, bright-colored, seemingly easy to spot. It doesn't work, but at least I try.

What does seem to work, and Deb is the one who thought of this, is tying a large, bright bow on the handle of the bag. Now, I'm a macho kinda guy so when Deb suggested this, I immediately raised my right eyebrow, kinda like the Rock does, and said, "I don't think so...." Well, she insisted that I try it. I did. It works! Every time! No matter which bag I take, as I said, they all look alike when they shoot out onto the carousel. But MINE has a large sparkly gold bow tied to the handle. No one else's does. I watch as others look at the name tags on the bags going by. I can spot mine 100 feet away. So simple and yet so effective. Thanks, Deb!

That's what works for me. The point is, mark your bags. That way you can get to the next part of your journey faster and with less stress.

Safe journey!

Where Did I Park?

You get off the plane, you get to the baggage claim area, wait for your bag that was the last one onto the carousel, get ready to head to the parking lot, and suddenly…PANIC! *Where are my keys?! I put them in my personal bag when I got here. But that bag is full of all the stuff I bought between leaving here and returning. WHERE ARE MY KEYS?!*

Now, now, clam down. (Notice how that admonishment always works?) *Let me think…. I didn't take them out during the trip so they must be at the bottom of my bag.* You stick your hand, maybe your arm, down through all the other stuff and, *Aghhh…, there they are.* The world isn't going to end after all. All is good…. But, WAIT! *Where did I park?* There's an app for that! No, really….

If you fly often, I suggest that you develop a parking routine. Always park in the same place, assuming you fly out of the same airport, of course. Right off hand, I can tell you where I park at DEN. I always park on the first floor and turn right where I look for a spot. The door is numbered 105/107. It's my routine. And it always works. But it didn't always work so easily.

Before I developed this routine, I was sure that I could remember where I'd parked. Come on, how could I not remember after only a few days. Well, let me tell you that it ain't old age…it's the altitude! Denver. Remember? One time I got home late and tired and, for the life of me, I couldn't remember where I'd parked my car. I knew it was on the first floor. I've always done that, but where on the first floor? I walked around, clicking the panic button on my fob, but could not locate it. It was embarrassing. After walking around for about a mile, a very nice lady in an official DEN Parking golf cart type vehicle stops me and asks me if I'm looking for my car. I acknowledge that I am. She asks me for the license plate number. It's HEIRPWR. I tell her that, she types it into her handy dandy device, and invites me to get into her vehicle. We go way over to the other side of the parking lot where she drops me off exactly in front of my car. I can't thank her enough. I'm so grateful. Now, I don't know that all airports provide that service but I know they do at DEN. And, I loaded the phone number onto my iPhone, just in case.

The key to getting through these dilemmas is, DON'T PANIC! Once panic strikes you, you can't think straight. Calm down. (There's that admonition again.) I've just given you a couple of things to consider to help you get to your car. As I said, there's an app for that. There are several, actually. I've tried them, but couldn't work them, so I just decided to develop my routine instead. Use what works for you and hope that when you get to the airport you don't see a sign as you approach the parking lot that says, "Closed. Under construction." If so, you're on your own…!

Safe journey!

Drop Off or Pick Up

If you're not the traveler, as you drive up to the airport, there will be only one of two reasons you're there, either you're dropping off someone, or picking up someone. There's a difference! In fact, there will be signs to try to help you. One of them says "Passenger Drop Off" and the other says "Passenger Pick Up." It's really quite simple. But, PLEASE, do your homework BEFORE you get to the airport. Go online and look at the maps provided so that you'll know where you're going. Chances are that it'll be fairly chaotic as you get to those signs. And most people will not be as conscientious as you, so they won't know which lane to take.

So, you've done your homework. You know your purpose. You see the signs. You take the correct lane. Now, do what the sign told you to do! Drop the person, or persons, off. Stop your car as close as you can to the correct door designated for their particular airline. Get out of the car with your passenger. Open the trunk. Take his or her bags out of the trunk. Say so long to the person. Get back in your car. Leave the area and the airport. Don't lollygag. You should have reminisced about the good times BEFORE leaving for the airport. There are hundreds of folks dropping people off. Get 'er done and get outta there. You'll have done a great service for a lot of folks. No one will thank you, except me, but they'll be grateful. Thank you!

Now, if you're picking someone up, do the same, or similar thing. Yeah, you have to greet and hug each other, but do it quickly. You're holding up the delay. Get 'em and get out.

If you're a rebel and don't like to take directions, nor like to follow them, don't fly! The directions given are important to follow because it's incredibly difficult to herd cats. And that's what all those people trying to get somewhere will be acting like. Be like a dog. Sit when told to sit. Drop off. Pick up. Move on. You'll appreciate others doing so. Do it yourself.

Safe journey!

Don't Do This

From a Flight Attendant

Don't take people's bags out of the bins to place your bag in. I had a passenger remove my bag one time, stuck it in the middle of the aisle, placed their bag in the bin. When I was walking up I asked who's bag was in the bin? The guy said, "It's mine." I asked, "So you removed this bag to place yours in it?" He said, "Yes, it was in my bin space and no one claimed it." I said, "No one claimed it because it's a 'crew bag.'" People think that the bins by their seat have to be where their bag goes. It doesn't. I know it's more convenient to have it by you, but it can't always happen that way. So, please don't move other bags. Ask a flight attendant for help. We will find a place for your bag.

Don't be Stupid!

There are plenty of places on land where you can make your stand about anything you choose. Please, don't do it on an airplane. It's dangerous! For you and for the other passengers. I believe in the First Amendment. In fact, I served in the military for fifty years volunteering to fight for your right as an American to say whatever you like. But not at the expense of others' lives, which is what you're doing if you do something stupid on an airplane. Here's the thing, those folks seated in that airplane with you are not your enemies. They're innocent bystanders at best. They don't know, and probably don't care, about your plight. Let them be. When you get to your destination safely, and everyone on board goes their merry way, then go protest all you want, but not on the plane. And that's all I have to say about that.

Safe journey!

This is the Captain speaking...

Here's some sage advice from my friend and former colleague, Eric Eklund.

1. Be early.
2. Don't back up without looking or you'll get run over.
3. Go to the bathroom before lining up for the flight.
4. Plan extra time to get something to eat before getting in line for the flight.
5. If someone asks, "Do you want to go to the club?".....the answer is Yes!
6. Always check the airport flight information screens.
7. Get the airline app and figure it out before getting to the airport.
8. Don't get up to leave the airplane until the row in front of you is moving off.
9. Put YOUR bag over YOUR seat.
10. Make eye contact and pay attention to the Flight Attendants, it will pay dividends.
11. Tell the Pilots thank you and offer chocolate.

Don't Talk to Your Neighbor

I know that you want to be kind and nice and courteous and all of those things, but maybe not today.... There are more than less times that I really don't want to chat with you. Sorry. Not sorry. I'm anxious about the flight. I'm anxious because I'm sure that I forgot something but can't remember what it is. I didn't make a list. I didn't get much sleep. I worked all day and want to chill out for a few hours on the way home. I'm old, therefore, cranky. There are myriad reasons for me not wanting to chat with you for the next three hours. Maybe it's you who feels this way. It's reciprocal.

Please, don't talk to me unless I want to talk to you. How will you know? I don't know. Listen to your eyes and your gut. Now, there are some folks who look as if they don't want to chat but won't stop once you get them going. Just pay attention. Experts say that the communication process is 90 percent-plus nonverbal. In other words, it's NOT the words, it's the expressions and other bodily movements that tell the truth about whether a person is having an exciting day or just wants to chill.

Maybe Etsy should offer a sign that we can purchase online that says, simply, "Please, leave me alone and don't talk to me." Try to read the signs and don't chat with me unless I'm up to it. Thank you! Now, please, excuse me while I take a nap....

Safe journey!

From a Flight Attendant

We're on this nice, lovely flight with this parrot. Okay, cool. My flying partner walks by the passenger later and looks down into the carrier. Yalllllll! It's a freaking CHICKEN! And the chicken has diapers! There is a freaking CHICKEN on my plane with diapers! How did a chicken get on my plane, and even more important, how the hell does one put a diaper on a freaking chicken?!

No Cell Phones, Please

As I write this, there's a lot of controversy about letting passengers talk on their cell phones while the aircraft is flying the sometimes friendly skies. I'm not an engineer or whatever it takes to make a trusted decision but I've always heard that the signals cell phones send through the sky can affect the electronics of an aircraft. I'm not sure I believe it, but I have no reason not to, except that I don't trust the airlines. Let's say, though, that that's all propaganda and using cell phones in flight will have no effect on the aircraft's ability to fly safely, okay? Here's what I DO know! I don't want it!

I don't want passengers talking on their cell phones during a flight. Can you imagine the cacophony they would create. People already talk way more loudly than they have to on their phones. I usually have to lower the volume on mine when I'm having a conversation. You don't have to yell! I think people do yell because when they have the phone up to their ear, or an earbud in their ear, it deadens the sound so that they think they have to speak louder than they do. I don't care to know what Aunt Hilda told Granma yesterday at dinner! I'm sorry for you, but if you have to go get tests done, go. We don't need to know that, and they're OBGYN tests?! NO! I don't want to hear it. Oh, but WAIT! What did you find your husband doing with your sister. I DO want to hear that!

Deb and I were having lunch in a public restaurant once when we overheard a lady tell whomever she was talking with on her cell phone what her social security number was. Yeah! The entire restaurant could hear her. That's what gets folks in trouble.

No, no, no! Please, airlines, for the love of God, don't allow passengers to crank up their phones during the flight. I really do need my beauty rest and the three-hour flight I'm about to take is the only place I can get that. It's bad enough that I have to listen to the movie their watching via their cranked up headphones.

Safe journey!

Are You Talkin' to ME?

I fly out of Denver International Airport (DEN) whenever I travel by air. There's an airport in Colorado Springs (COS), which is a few miles closer and more convenient in a way. A lot fewer people travel through there. But there are a lot less flights going out of there too. I usually fly on business which means I have to get to my destination on time. I speak for a living. My hosts expect me to be there, so I usually fly out to where I'm going a day ahead. It makes me and my hosts more comfortable that I'm there a day ahead of the event for which they've hired me to speak. If you don't catch the ONE flight out of COS, you're dead. Sorry, not literally. Not sorry. Anyway, there are always a lot of people at DEN. A LOT! I read somewhere that 20,000 people travel through DEN every hour. WOW! Although, I wonder, "Who counted?"

Anyway, this has happened several times. You'd think that I'd learn better. Evidently, I haven't. They always get me. It just happened the last time I flew. I'm standing at my gate (I stand for a few minutes before boarding because I know I'll be sitting for a long time. Gets the blood flowing through my legs, feet, and toes. Which are protected by closed-toe shoes, by the way.) when a person approaches me and starts chatting with me. "Hey, how are you doing?" he'll ask. "Fine," I reply, "Thank you. And you?" "It's been a while since we talked so I wanted to reach out to you to make sure that all is well," he replies. I've never seen this person in my life, but a lot of people whom I don't know, know me. They may have studied with me, heard one of my talks or podcasts, or something. I'm in front of a lot of people, all who think I remember them. I don't. So, I'm thinking that this guy talking to me must know me from some event. I just hope that I don't owe him money. "Thanks," I reply. Suddenly, he turns away from me as he keeps talking. I can't understand what he's saying. That's when I see it. The ear bud. He's talking to someone else on his phone. Not to me.

I've had "conversations" with folks that have lasted ten or fifteen minutes. Them talking to someone else. Me answering them. Now, America is still a free country. At least while I'm typing. People can, and do, whatever they want to do. But the courteous thing to do is to not lead people on. They think you're being nice when you're not. Here's what I suggest. Put your phone up to your ear. That way people (I) know that you're talking to someone who's not there. And don't yell. Everyone can hear you. Especially when you're sharing something personal that the entire world should not hear about until it's on CNN.

The airport isn't the friendliest place in the world. It's not Disneyland. So it's nice to find someone friendly enough to talk with you. I know I appreciate that. But be sincere with who you're talking to. Talk face to face. High touch is always better than high tech.

Safe journey!

Don't Cut the Line

Look, whether you agree or not, or even realize it or not, there's a process each airline has researched and decided that works best for them to board their passengers onto the plane. Like you, I wonder why they don't do it as you or I would do it. It'd be a lot better and more efficient, but they won't ask us. That just stinks. In the meantime, go by their process. Mumble loudly as you go up the tunnel, but follow the process. And DON'T CUT THE LINE!

If you're supposed to be in Group 4 for boarding, wait until the previous groups have been called and boarded. If you're in Group 5, it just really sucks to be you, but that doesn't give you license to cut the line. Don't do it!

I wish that I could tell you that the Boarding Manager (I just made that up.) will stop you, but I've never seen it happen. They'll usually just let you through. They don't care that much to confront you. But I could be wrong! They may be armed. They may secretly work for TSA and they're looking for line cutters to do bodily harm to. It could happen. And you know that.

Worse, other passengers in the queue may discover that you're not in their group and take the law into their own hands. God knows what they might do to you. Some folks are attention seekers and will do anything to go viral on social media. I just wouldn't take a chance.

Please, be courteous and take your turn when boarding. Don't cut the line. Your seat will be there when you get on the plane. Now will there be any room to store your oversized carry on? That's another story….

Safe journey!

Where's the Bathroom?

I'm what many call a motivational speaker as well as a writer and educator, but mostly a wisdom seeker and storyteller. You may remember a great leader by the name of Colin Powell. People used to tell me that I resembled him when I wore my glasses. I took it as a compliment and even included it as part of my presentations. You can Google both of us and decide for yourself if we ever looked alike.

I'll get back to that in a moment. I have no idea what sort of attraction I have for people at the airport but I do have a question. Of all the thousands of people travelling through the airport on any given day, why do they come up to ME to ask me where the bathroom is? First of all, the airport is the first place everyone should practice Situational Awareness. Crazy things can, and do, happen at airports. We all owe it to ourselves and to each other to pay attention to what's going on and report anything that seems suspicious. I'm sorry that it's that way any more, but it's the way of the world now.

Situational Awareness doesn't just mean watching for others' behaviors, it also means noticing where things are. Like the bathrooms! They have signs! Even images to depict the gender of people allowed in them. Look around and stop coming up to me, of all people, and asking me where the bathrooms are! "Sir, do you know where the bathroom is?" "NO! I'm from New Mexico! I pee outside!" Come on, man....

But they do it. The other day, there was a LITTLE bit of a change up. A guy came up to me to ask me where gate A36 was. "First of all," I told him, "this is terminal C. You're not even close. Get back on the tram and ride it to terminal A. Get off of it there and ask someone else." I really was trying to be helpful, but I didn't know. I was just a confused pax, like him. I was actually looking for the bathroom when he asked me. Ironic, ha?

I was in San Juan, Puerto Rico, speaking one time and was at a public park with the VIPs that I was supposed to address the next day when a man came up and asked me where the bathrooms were. In Spanish. I guess I look Puerto Rican enough for folks to assume that I speak Spanish. I do. I still didn't know where the bathrooms were, though. Three people who must have overheard the man ask me came up to me, as well, and asked me the same thing. ¡Yo no se!

Back to Colin Powell. As I would ask my audiences...What would you do if you saw Colin Powell at the airport? Since you're too young to know who he is, substitute Jason Momoa's name. I mean, you see him (Me/Jason) and you want to go speak to him. How would you do that without sounding like a silly fan? You'd ask him where the bathroom is! That's an innocent enough question. Then you can ask for an autograph and a photo op. I would do it for you....

If you see a tall, Ruggedly Handsome gentleman just minding his own business at the airport, please don't come up to me and ask me where the bathroom is. There are maps throughout the airport. Look there first. Or, better yet, look around for a sign!

Safe journey!

On the Plane

From a Flight Attendant

When masks were in place it was awful with tattle tales! I don't know how many adults would buzz me or tell me while doing my service. The worse one was when I had a lady traveling with her daughter who had Down Syndrome and looked to be the age of four. The little girl's mask had fallen off and I clearly saw the mom getting one out of her bag to put on her. There was a lady right behind the mother as I walked by who grabbed me and said the mother was not making her daughter put her mask on. I really wanted to smack that woman. Lol. I'm like, "Ma'am, she is currently working on it." But then the little girl was playing with the mask during the flight and that lady kept telling me to tell the mother to make her wear it. We were NOT mask police. I really wanted to toss the tattle tale lady off the plane.

Don't Remove Your Shoes

Surely, your mother taught you that taking your shoes off in other people's presence is rude and nasty. If she didn't, then let me tell you that **taking your shoes off in other people's presence is rude and nasty! Especially in a confined area like an airplane!** You're welcome.

Yeah, you bathed before you left your house to go to the airport. That was eight hours ago. Oh yeah, it was 102 degrees between your house and the airport. Hmmmm…. Might you, AND your feet, have sweated a little bit in between. Is it possible your feet now stink of sweat among possibly other things? Possible. Please, give every passenger in the plane the benefit of the doubt and **DO NOT TAKE YOUR SHOES OFF IN THE PLANE!**

And, please, consider wearing closed-toe shoes. Maybe some passengers will appreciate seeing your toes, especially your newly polished toenails that you paid a lot to have done and want to impress everyone with, but most, you'll have to trust me, don't care. Instead of making a positive impression it'll be a totally negative impression. No one will tell you, but that's the truth. Again, you're welcome!

So, please, for the sake of humanity, keep your toes covered. BTW, Crocks don't count as shoes….

Safe journey!

From a Flight Attendant

We get yelled at so much over silly things, stowing bags, cell phone calls, or when a passenger falls asleep and we pass them by in service. They catch such attitudes like we passed them by on purpose. I don't wake people.

Words From the Cockpit

I mentioned how you won't be able to understand the announcements from the Gate Keepers. Well, you probably won't understand the captain either. If they were trained to speak into those microphones, they probably got the same training, because they sound the same. I'm reminded of the teacher on Peanuts cartoons, "Wah, wah, wah, wah...."

I assume that the captains have never heard their own voice as they welcome their passengers or pass on important information. If they did, they might work on their enunciation and other specific methods for communicating.

Now, to their credit, they're usually speaking over the plane's engines, which makes it difficult to understand what they're saying. But an announcer's voice is different than a normal speaking voice.

I'm not dissing them, just making an observation. Trying to help, really....

Safe journey!

bob vásquez

Flight Attendants Are People Too

Aldous Huxley said that, "We shall know the truth and it shall make us mad." Well, I'm not sure I'm mad, but I DO have a different view of flight attendants based on what I learned from Angie and some of her peers.

Am I alone or don't most of us have this perception of flight attendants that they must make a lot of money, they're worldly, cool, almost-celebrities? Okay, I'm the only one. Well, evidently, they're people too! Yeah, I didn't know that either until my niece, Angie, straightened me out. Here's some of what she taught me.

"Most Flight Attendants struggle to make ends meet, I made $27,000 last year. Even though my hourly pay is $31.00 right now, we don't get hourly pay for boarding, it starts when the main cabin door closes and then ends when it opens. We are only guaranteed to work 75 hours a month."

I've flown enough to know that flight attendants' jobs begin way before that cabin door closes. And they deserve way more than what a McDonald's employee makes. Okay, McDonald's employees make less than $31.00, but not much less. They certainly don't have the responsibilities and headaches flight attendants deal with EVERY flight! I can't remember flight attendants going on strike, but if they ever do, I'm behind them all the way!

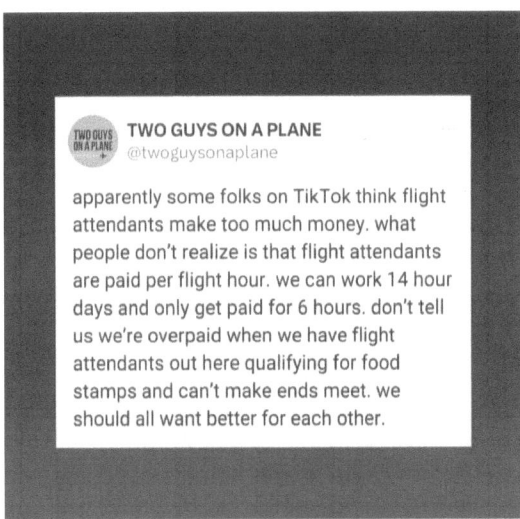

Here are Angie's thoughts when I asked her why she and her fellow flight attendants do it.

"Is it worth it? Yes and no. I struggle to make ends meet sometimes but I absolutely love it! Yes, I could go back to banking, working 40 hours a week at $20.00 an hour and be okay financially, but I wouldn't enjoy going to work."

"Why do I do it? Because of the love and passion I feel when I do fly. I was happy in banking for the 20 years that I did it, at least I thought I was. But it's a different mindset and feeling I have when I do this job. I love meeting new people, I love the adventure. The majority do it for the benefits, but I just love talking with people and seeing where they are going or why. It just gives me so much happiness.

"The first year was rough and I questioned myself about what I was thinking. I walked away from

27 paid vacation days, 12 paid holidays off, making 48k a year, home every night and weekend. But everyone said give it a year. And they were right. It's a different kind of lifestyle and I love it. I wish I did international though, but maybe one day. But for now, I just love the places I get to see. I would have loved being in the military but I knew I was too sensitive and wasn't sure I could live up to the physical part of it or living outside and I'm afraid of bugs. Travel seems so cliché to use as to why I love it so much but it's a big part of it.

"I recall one Christmas Eve heading to Allentown PA for a layover. A gentleman came on board. I could tell he was broken. I bent down by his side. He was sitting with his wife. I asked him if he was okay and if I could get him something. For me, seeing a grown man cry wasn't something you witness daily. His wife shared that he was heading home to plan his dad's funeral. He shared with me that he had just talked to him two days prior. It wasn't expected. I gave the man a hug and got him some water. During the flight I wrote him a card. When I went up to him during the flight, I shared with him that I'd lost my mom. We shared some tears together. I told him to read the card when he was ready. At the end of the flight, the couple sat on the plane until everyone was gone. He wanted to thank me for being kind. They had exchanged numbers with my flying partner. The next morning when we flew out, my partner had me hang back before security. The couple had showed up with a Christmas card. They had given me a gift in the card. Made my Christmas.

"Another reason I do what I do…. I was carrying a passenger to bury a loved one, I've carried passengers going to meet a grand baby, or a parent going to see a graduation. It's being part of life-moments that just warm my heart and soul."

THANK YOU all of our flight attendants! We probably don'ts say it, nor show it, enough, but we appreciate you!

Safe journey!

Don't Touch the Flight Attendants

I asked a few of my friends who are pilots and flight attendants for commercial airlines what they might commend you to do or to not do and I was flabbergasted by how many mentioned, "Don't touch the Flight Attendants!"

You'd think that in this day and age when EVERYTHING is recorded and shared online, that people, especially men, would have more respect for others than to touch them disrespectfully in public. Let me tell you, flying commercially is not a private endeavor. It's very public. And unlike the "What happens in Vegas...." perspective, "What happens on your flight is subject to be the lead story on tonight's evening news."

DO NOT, I'll repeat, DO NOT touch the flight attendants, male or female! *Oh, but I didn't do it on purpose*. My niece, Angie, tells me that, often, that toucher will excuse themselves the first time and say that it wasn't intentional. But when it happens three or four times, that's intentional. Don't do it!

I have to commend flight attendants for their appearance. They all look very attractive and professional, at least when they get to the gate. I've seen some that didn't look so good after the flight because of the crazies flying that day. Would you go up and touch a bank teller? Or your doctor?

Guys...! I won't admonish gals because I don't know if they think like us guys, I've never been one. Guys...! They're not flirting with you! Yeah, that's a common fantasy. It's a job (or profession). It's their business. You're not that good looking. Present company accepted, of course. Be respectful. Don't touch them!

Safe journey!

What to Wear

Back in the day, there was an expectation that passengers would wear nice clothes on their flight. Maybe their "Sunday best." I remember having to get dressed up to some degree before heading to the airport. Not anymore! As more and more people began flying commercially, that expectation dwindled into what it is today...anything goes...or very little goes.

In my feeble mind, I'm thinking that you have two choices: being respectful (to yourself and fellow passengers) or trying to get attention (of your passengers).

Up until recently, there was an expectation for professionals to dress for success. Then we decided that looking like a bum is professional. Okay, that was a side thought. You know what I mean if you've watched the news lately.

Anyway, what you wear to the airport and onto the plane says a lot about whether or not you respect yourself. Showing off what you don't have or too much of what you DO have is disrespectful to yourself. Yeah, America is still a free country, and you're free to disrespect yourself as much as you choose, but keep that in mind as you select what you'll wear to the airport and onto the plane. Although your rationalization has to do with your personal freedom, notice that you'll be influencing others. You have no choice in that. You WILL influence others. The choice is whether it'll be in a positive or negative way. You choose. People will say, "WOW! Look at that beautiful person. Doesn't have to show off!" Or they'll say,

"WOW! Look at that gross looking person. Poor thing. There's gotta be help for that."

Whether or not you're a social media influencer, very rich, a celebrity, whatever, be respectful to yourself and others. Cover up what needs covering up. If you're looking for attention, which is why, I think, people wear the grotesque clothing that they do a lot of time, you can do that by being kind and courteous. THAT's attractive to EVERYONE! And it'll go even beyond your flight.

Safe journey!

Don't Lock Yourself in the Lavatory

My grandson, five-years-old, locked himself in the toilet on a flight not long ago. He was traumatized. You can imagine. Now, know that the correct term for a toilet on an airplane is "lavatory." You should know that so that you know what the flight attendant giving the Safety Briefing is referring to.

My best advice is, DON'T lock yourself in the lavatory so that you can't get out. If you do, don't panic. Knock on the door until a flight attendant hears you, at which time he or she will do what it takes to unlock the door. It's a secret how they do it, but know that they can and will. Just be patient. And when they DO let you out, say THANK YOU!

Safe journey!

From a Flight Attendant

Pets are another one we get a lot of heat on. I love dogs! But pets have to be stowed during taxi, take-off, and landing. That's the policy. And they have to remain in their carrier the entire flight. But we have people that will try and wrap them up like babies, thinking that we won't notice or say anything, or they argue over seatbelt extenders in the emergency row. We have people who bring their own extenders and sit in the emergency row because they want more room. Then when we have to simply say it's not allowed, they act like it's the plane's seatbelt.

Close Your Window

I may have already admonished you to be courteous and kind. Please, do that. One way you will is by closing your window, if you're in a window seat, as appropriate.

I like the window seat. There's a window next to it! Amazing, ha?! But I try to be aware of what's happening around me so that I open or close the window so that it doesn't affect my fellow passengers in a negative way.

Sometimes, you'll want to close your window when the sun is shining in at an angle or with such brightness that it will blind you or your row-mates. Sometimes, you'll want to open it to shed some light into the cabin (the part of the plane where you and your fellow travelers sit) so that it brightens the environment. And you can open it a little bit or completely. Sometimes, a little bit is enough.

In my culture we have a physical admonition that's called, "El Ojo." The Eye. If someone gives you El Ojo, that's not a good thing. You don't even have to be Latino to realize that you just messed up and that you should correct yourself immediately. If you open your little window and your row-mate(s) gives you El Ojo, please consider closing it. That probably means that the light shining in is too bright. Again, be courteous and kind. You have every right to open or close your window as you choose, but remember that there are others riding with you. Sometimes your right may not be right.

Safe journey!

This is the Captain speaking...

Here's some advice from my good friend and pilot extraordinaire, Rich Mandeville.

Listen to the Flight Attendants' safety briefing. Glance at the exit nearest you and look at the emergency card for once. And if it gets bad enough to evacuate, forget your stuff and hustle out. Everything else we can laugh at later. Nothing else matters to your family waiting for your arrival/return.

And get to the airport early...who needs stress? Pack lightly. Smile at your fellow row-mates. Say thank you and please to the crew. Buckle up. Enjoy the ride!

Don't Kick the Seat

PLEASE, PLEASE, PLEASE, DON'T KICK THE BACK OF THE SEAT IN FRONT OF YOU. Now, if you can kick the back of the seat behind you, let me know. Cirque du Soleil may have a spot for you.

You can argue all you want about who that seat back belongs to, but think about it objectively. The back of the seat is attached to the actual seat in front of you. Someone paid to sit in it. It belongs to them. Don't kick it. Intentionally, anyway. Sometimes, you can't help but kick it. When that happens, apologize sincerely and try not to do it again.

I usually think that kids are the worse culprits at this. Not necessarily. I was on a two-hour flight recently on which an adult woman kept kicking the back of my seat. I did what I could, giving her El Ojo, sighing, you know, all the typical things we do instead of confronting the person. Nowadays, confronting someone can lead to huge arguments and even fights, so I avoid that if I can. It shouldn't be that way, but it is.

In trying to be understanding, I know that some folks have nervous ticks that lead a person to tap on things, like the back of the seat in front of you. Please be aware that you're affecting, maybe even pissing off, the person in front of you.

And if you ARE traveling with a Little, please ensure that he or she doesn't kick the seat. I know that may be difficult, but it's the right thing. It teaches that Little self restraint and respect. Two important characteristics that will help him or her become a good citizen. Thanks for raising a good kid! Safe journey!

Don't Hoard the Armrest

Unless you're sitting in First Class, you'll have to deal with who gets the armrest between your seat and your neighbor's. I don't really know if there's a rule or rules. Here's what I suggest.

If you're siting in seats labeled A, B, or C, go toward the left. The A seats will be the window seats. If you're seated in an A seat, there will be an armrest to the left of your seat. That one's yours. No argument. The one to your right, is to the left of the person in the B seat. That's primarily their armrest. The armrest to the right of that seat is to the left of the C seat, which is the aisle seat. That's primarily theirs. Yes, that means that the aisle seat gets two armrests. Pick the aisle seat if you want two armrests. This also goes for seats D, E, and F, only to the right instead of the left. The F seat will be the window seat. I didn't want to type all of that all over again. Sorry.

As I often say, be courteous and kind. If you HAVE to rest your arm on the armrest that's not yours, ask your fellow passenger if it's okay to use it. It very well may be. A lot of us try to sleep during the flight. We probably won't need the armrest for that. And, often, the armrest is long enough to accommodate two elbows, one toward the front of the armrest and one toward the back. You can easily negotiate that agreeably.

This may seem like a trivial issue, but it can easily escalate. Once more, be courteous and kind. It'll go a long way. And you may need that if you're going a long way.

Safe journey!

This is the Captain speaking…

My Little Brother and experienced pilot, Rob Barkers, says….

Respect your seat mates, respect other passengers, respect the Flight Attendants. Overall, respect! We're a carbon fiber tube for a period of time and it may be uncomfortable, but we're all in it together.

Wear Headphones

If you're going to watch a movie or music videos or TikTok videos or whatever, either on your device or the plane's device, please, wear headphones or earpods. You can blow your ears out if you like. This is America and I fought for 50 years to give you that right. But don't make me hear what you're listening to. And not at the volume that you listen to it. Thank you! Safe journey!

From a Flight Attendant

Half the support animals we don't even think are real nowadays! You can buy the stuff anywhere including Amazon. You can tell which ones are real and not due to how they act. And people try and let their pets out and run up and down the aisle. It's crazy some days. I love animals but it's a bit much these days.

If You're Taking a Pet

All of a sudden, everyone's got some kind of support animal that they have to travel with. It's gotten ridiculous! To the point that those who really do have and need a support animal are lumped in with those who are doing it for...well, for their own reasons.

In 1996 and in 2002, when my family and I flew to and from Germany we had to put our dogs in carriers and they were stowed with the baggage. They survived. I don't know that that's the most humane way for them to fly, but sometimes I wonder if how I barely fit in that seat in the cabin is humane.

Now, don't get all curled up like a snake and think that I'm a pet hater. I'm not. It's just that, like so many things, some folks take advantage of a valid break for others and pretty soon it gets out of hand.

Deb and I recently flew on a flight on which a young lady had a Husky with her. It had the official vest and everything so we're pretty sure that it was a bona fide support dog. Man, I wish he was MY dog. We didn't even know he was there! He crawled under the owner's seat in front of her, never made a sound, and followed her every command. Not a problem.

But I've also flown with the little yapper in the purse! Worse than kids crying. I'm pretty sure that wasn't supposed to happen. Now, if the flight attendants try to enforce the rules, it'll quickly turn chaotic. And it'll be recorded for TikTok.

If you have to have a support animal, a donkey, an alligator, what have you, please follow the rules. The airlines will tell you what those are. Don't put the flight attendants in a bad situation. They're just trying

to do their job of keeping you and all your fellow passengers safe.
Safe journey!

Where's My Bag?

In another story, I refer to marking your bag so that you can claim it easily. But that's if it arrives with you. It may, or may not. I'm not sure how it works, or doesn't, but there might be a time that your bags decide to take a different flight than the one you're on. It happens. But you won't know it happened until it's too late. Like when you need it and it ain't there.

If you have an important appointment or event to attend when you arrive at your destination, I highly recommend that you take a carry-on with you that includes everything that you'll need for that appointment or event. You're welcome!

Know that your bags are expendable. They'll be thrown around and possibly destroyed. I was sitting in my window seat once when I happened to look out at the conveyor belt that the baggage handlers were throwing bags onto to load underneath the plane. I do mean throwing them. I'm not going to accuse anyone of doing so intentionally, but as they threw a leather-looking suitcase onto that belt, it burst open. All kinds of clothes and stuff flew out of it. The handlers were going nuts trying to capture everything as they tried to stuff it back into the suitcase to no avail. The person seated behind me was yelling, "That's my bag!" and trying to get the flight attendant to do something about it. They tried, but I couldn't tell that they succeeded. She was pretty torqued. I would have been too!

One last thing on bags. Don't carry what you're not supposed to! Every airline website and app will provide you a detailed list of what you can, and what you can't, pack in your bags. Please, follow those directions! I read this online just the other day:

"It is disappointing to continue to see travelers carrying their loaded guns to our security checkpoints," John Busch, TSA's federal security director at Reagan National, said. "My advice is that when packing for a flight to start with a completely empty bag, and all travelers must pack their own bag, so that there are no surprises when someone gets to our checkpoint."

This statement was in reference to a guy who had a gun in one of his bags. His excuse was that his wife had packed it for him. Sure…. Whatever…. I wonder if they're still married….
Safe journey!

Aisle or Window Seat?

Which came first, the chicken of the egg? I've pondered that for decades, usually while I'm sitting on an airplane that's sitting on the tarmac and probably not moving for a while. Another question I ponder, but this usually as I plan a trip, is whether I should pick the window or aisle seat? I don't know any adult who prefers the middle seat. So that question is answered rather quickly. But should I select the window or aisle seat? THAT is the question! Take that, Shakespeare!

I usually prefer the window seat. I like to look out to see where we might be when you can see beyond the clouds and in daylight. You also get to see the sights. I was on a flight from southern California to Denver one morning that flew right over Monument Valley across Arizona and Utah. It was spectacular! A beautiful smooth clear flight, it was like a National Geographic video. I can still feel the exhilaration that I felt appreciating what the Creator has gifted us. Back in the day, the Captain used to be a tour guide. It was always a male back then and he'd tell us to look to the right and see so-and-so, or to the left as we flew past so-and-so. That doesn't happen anymore. I guess that there's an app for that.

The window seat also allows you to look out for storms, not that you can do anything about them, but maybe brace yourself for them, or start praying. I also like the window seat because I can lean against the side of the plane as I nod off. It's not exactly comfortable, but if you have a small pillow it's better than leaning onto the passengers next to you or falling into the aisle. Not that I've ever done that....

I'm sitting in the aisle seat because that's what was left when I booked the flight. It's not a long flight so I figure that I can put up with any inconvenience. If you're an aisle seater you're asking, "What inconvenience?" Well, I've got fairly long legs. And I can't afford the seats that give you enough room to keep your knees out of the aisle. So, as I sit there and I lose my bearing, my knee falls out toward the aisle. And guess what part of the flight we're in the middle of? The part where the flight attendants roll those beverage carts up and down the aisle! BAM! I'm gonna give the flight attendants the benefit of the doubt and say that they don't smash into my knee on purpose. But can't they see it! Yeah, they've got more important things to do like pass out those little liquor bottles. Either way, my knee ends up all bruised up. No aisle seat for me, please.

Oh, and if I'm "lucky" enough to board with Group One or Two and I'm already seated in that aisle seat, I get banged up by people who have a different perspective of what a carry-on looks like than the airline does. (Read my story about carry-ons.) Again, I know everyone has more important things going on than worrying about banging their carry-on into my shoulder, like where they're going to put that trunk since they ended up in Group 4 and the overhead compartments are already full.

Life is a choice. Choose wisely. You'll eventually develop a preference. In the meantime, consider others' knees and shoulders as you board the plane, won't you? Thanks in advance.

Safe journey!

Turbulence

No matter what, there's always a possibility of going through some turbulence. There are four levels of turbulence: Light, Moderate, Severe, and Extreme. It's often referred to as bumpiness. Now, I'm telling you this not to scare you, but to inform you.

There are many turbulence apps that will provide you information about where it may be lighter or heavier. I look at those sites to prepare myself, more or less. They're not always perfectly accurate, though, and turbulence can pop up out of nowhere.

My protégé, Stiggy, who's been a pilot for a long time says this: "Turbulence isn't as bad as you think, especially if you keep your seatbelt fastened. Modern aircraft can handle turbulence really well and the planes won't fall apart, no need to worry much. We're also not supposed to fly through severe thunderstorms, which helps quite a bit, so we try to avoid them as much as possible."

One of my mentors who is known as THE Captain says, "Don't be afraid and, no, the wings won't fall off in turbulence!"

There you have it. Don't worry, be happy.

If you do happen to hit some bumps along your flight, please, don't yell, scream, or panic! If it gets bad enough to warrant panicking you don't need to feed the chaos by yelling and screaming. It doesn't do any good. If you must to do something, which is a human thing, pray. The flight attendants, the pilots, and your fellow passengers aren't going to do anything to alleviate the bumps. But God might.

My Chosen Brother and pilot, Sean, says, "When the airplane encounters turbulence, people open their window shade. 9.9 times out of 10 you will see nothing (especially in a cloud, where turbulence happens often). In addition, even with sophisticated equipment and air traffic, it's hard to predict where it is and how long it will last." Again, don't panic.

What bothers me when we hit bumps is the lack of control. I can't do anything about it but hang on and have faith that the pilots, the crew, and the plane remain viable. My faith and trust are tested. I pray a lot….

Safe journey!

The Value of Duct Tape

This is a true story.

I'm sitting in an airplane on the tarmac at Denver International Airport. I don't remember when this is occurring, but it's summertime. It's hot. We usually get a week of really hot temps in Colorado. It used to be the first week of August. So, it's the first week of August in Colorado and I'm sitting in an airplane on the tarmac at Denver International Airport....

After sitting on the tarmac for about an hour, the pilot comes onto the intercom and apologizes, of course, and informs us that the plane has a maintenance issue that must be corrected before we can take off. He reminds us that safety is the most important part of flying with his airline. Yeah, yeah.... It's still very hot and the A/C that's on isn't working very well. IT'S HOT, I TELL YA!

Another fifteen minutes pass. Suddenly, a flight attendant is summoned to the cockpit via a couple of dings. I know this because I hear the dings. A flight attendant marches from the back of the plane into the cockpit and closes the door. We're still waiting and it's still hot. Getting hotter, actually. A few minutes later, that same flight attendant from the back of the plane comes out of the cockpit with a huge roll of duct tape in her hands. No kidding. This is a true story. I wouldn't lie to you. She marches, and I do mean marches. I was an Air Force Bandsman for 24 years. I know what marching looks like. She marches down the aisle to the back of the plane to a door that had been opened a few minutes prior to let air flow through the cabin to cool it off a little. Most people aren't paying any attention to all of this, but I am.

The flight attendant talks to someone outside the airplane and hands them the big roll of duct tape. No kidding. About ten minutes later, the flight attendant closes the door, talks to someone on the plane's phone, then the pilot comes onto the intercom with good news. The plane is fixed! We're ready to go! And we start to taxi toward the runway. Obviously, I survived the flight.

Now, I'm not sure if this was all coincidence or a miracle. Albert Einstein once said that, "We can live our lives in one of two ways, as if there are no such things as miracles or as if everything is." Miracle or not, I know what I saw and I'm reporting it to you now. We sometimes make fun of the uses and value of duct tape, but I know the truth! And now you do too!

Safe journey!

Kids are People Too

You'll be lucky if there arc no little kids on your flight. Especially if they're not happy. I don't know what makes kids unhappy when they fly. I mean, they have their parents' full attention. They usually even sit on the parents' laps the entire flight. They have new toys that their parents purchased for them specifically for the flight, brand new toys that will keep them happy. Supposed to, anyway…. The parents provide all of the snacks they want. I don't know why they'd be unhappy. But they are. Not all of them. Just the ones on the flight where you thought you might get some sleep. Ain't happening! And if you sit in front of the Kickers, the ones that have to kick the back of your seat incessantly….

What are you to do about it? Well, you can address the parents. If you're really lucky, the parents will understand that their kids are causing you and everyone else on the plane a certain amount of distress. As little as that tyke may be, his voice is amplified by the design of the cabin. There are engineers paid to make sure that all of the surfaces amplify the sound of a screaming child. They make a lot of money, I hear.

In my experience, the parents can do all they want. The kid is gonna scream! Maybe she's heard that saying about everyone screaming for ice cream? Nonetheless, some, maybe most, parents will try their best to entertain Jr so that he focuses on those new toys. That would make everyone happy.

But, you know, this is the first time that Missy has ever traveled by plane. There's nothing really to see out the window. You can't count license plates from New York or play I Spy. Getting ticked off at them only gets you more ticked off. You're not going to quiet the kid down. Nope. I know, I know, you paid for your ticket. You have the right to have a quiet flight. But kids are people too. Whatever it is that's spooked the baby, it has. If you can figure out what that is and alleviate it, tell the parents. If not, try to stay calm. Now's a good time to practice meditating. If you can meditate with all that going on, make sure that your yoga mates and your sensei know it. You get extra credit in heaven for doing so. No, really, you do!

That crying child doesn't know any better. Poor kid. Put yourself in their place. Put yourself in the parents' place. It's a lose/lose situation. Don't make it worse for them or for yourself. As that famous meme says, "Be Calm."

Be kind. Yeah, it may be difficult. But you don't know what the parents nor the children have been through or are going through. Traveling, especially by air, can be scary, especially the first time. Especially for LIttles. Try to put yourself in their place. How would you like your fellow travelers to react? Act accordingly.

Safe journey!

Making Connections

Your flight Is due to land at a particular time. Don't count on it. It may be on time. It may be early. It may be late.

If it arrives early, there's a chance that you'll be delayed on the tarmac due to another aircraft being at the gate that your plane is supposed to disembark at. That's reasonable. YOU'RE early. They're trying to take off on time. Waiting a little bit shouldn't bother you. As long as it's a little bit. Don't count on that!

If you're on time, you'd think that everything would be hunky dory. Maybe. Maybe not. I don't know how you'll select the flights you take. I like to take direct flights so that I don't have to worry about making connections, or worse, missing connections. If I have to make a connection, I'd rather spend as little time as possible wherever I'm laid over. I don't intentionally look at having to rush to make my connection, but sometimes that happens. And it always seems that I have to go to the other end of the airport to catch that next flight. All that to say this. If you know that someone around you, especially behind you, has a very short time to make their connection, please, let them go ahead of you! Help them out by staying in your seat, at least out of the aisle, so that they can get their stuff and head out of the plane as quickly as possible. I've seen folks intentionally get in the way of someone who's rushing to make a connection. That stinks! There's no room for rudeness on a plane. None! We're all trying to get somewhere and some times we have to rush to get

there. Please, be kind and help each other! You'd want others to do so for you.
Safe journey!

Travel time....

More books by Bob Vásquez! All available on amazon.com and in Apple Books.

  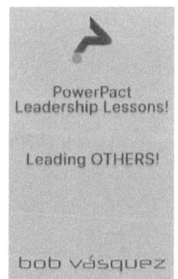

  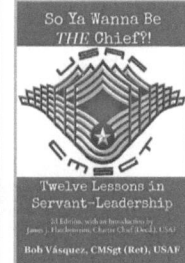

bob vásquez

Made in United States
Troutdale, OR
03/27/2025

30111249R00076